THE TOWER

GORDON BOSTIC

Primix Publishing
East Brunswick Office Evolution
1 Tower Center Boulevard, Ste 1510
East Brunswick, NJ 08816
www.primixpublishing.com
Phone: 1-800-538-5788

Published by Primix Publishing: 11/13/2024

ISBN: 979-8-88703-424-9(sc)
ISBN: 979-8-88703-425-6(e)

Library of Congress Control Number: 2024917442

CONTENTS

THE TOWER

The Tower stood for untold years
But never occupied.
And it seemed to have no purpose
When logic was applied.

With no clue to its origin
It mostly was ignored.
As there had been none brave enough,
It had gone unexplored.

Some said that since the world began
The Tower always stood.
Which they'd no way to verify
Nor sure they even should.

The war destroyed its history.
What little there had been.
So it had been a mystery
To state that it was in.

It clearly stood the test of time
Despite what it endured.
As though something protected it
So, safety was ensured.

Though around it all was rubble,
The Tower stood unscathed.
While they're many who suspicioned
In evil it had bathed.

Now it stood amidst a wasteland
Of ruin and debris.
What once had been the pinnacle
Of their society.

While many tales were told of it.
Some passed down through the years.
There're none that had been hesitant
To outline stress and fears.

There were rumors it was haunted
As sometimes late at night
Some claimed from it would emanate
A strange and eerie light.

THE WAR

What all had thought unthinkable
Exactly what occurred.
When man in his insanity
Destruction had assured.

The world reduced to a wasteland
Where few were left alive.
And those struggled in jeopardy
In effort to survive.

The war had only served to prove
How foolish man could be.
In believing a solution
War proved a remedy.

Where man in his insanity
Had let destruction rain.
With no regard for humankind
And little there to gain.

It all was over in a flash—
One brilliant blast of light.
Where war erupted by surprise
With few a chance at flight.

Beyond destruction that was wrought
Had been the grotesque change.
As it had left an afterworld
That had grown very strange.

THE AFTER WORLD

When from their bunkers they emerged
To a world laid to waste.
To face a new reality
That none wished to have faced.

They had termed it the After World
For all that had been left
Were remnants of society
Where justice was bereft.

Their new world was now a wasteland
So, they'd denote the change.
With ev'rything derived from war
Had been foreign and strange.

Now with cities nonexistent
All left were tribes and clans.
Those who'd bound themselves together
Devoid of other plans.

The churches were now all empty
As faith had disappeared.
The war had put an end to faith
As faith just interfered.

Society an afterthought
As so few had remained.
Where there was no law and order
Nor justice was obtained.

It was a world of dog-eat-dog
With most food stores destroyed.
So those fighting for survival
Used any means employed.

The world became a savage place
With the end of the war.
For survival had meant morals
Had been needed no more.

Whatever creatures were not killed
Had through mutation changed.
Where those who once had been demure
Had now become deranged.

Even vegetation dangerous
In struggle to survive.
For it seemed in the aftermath
Plant life had come alive.

It seemed that nature in response
Decided to strike back.
For ev'rything that was benign
Had now gone on attack.

Man's no longer a predator
But had become the prey.
For lost without technology
He'd also lost his way.

For in the struggle to survive
It had become quite plain
Man forfeited his position
At top of the food chain.

ZACK WILLIAMS

Zack Williams was a nobody
That most chose to ignore.
For he'd been a custodian
For years before the war.

Zack was truly nothing special
Who'd been caught out of place.
The rest were clearly brainiacs
While he just absorbed space.

Zack was no one of importance,
And thus an afterthought.
The people who surrounded him
Gave him no second thought.

His encampment was a hodgepodge
Of brains and engineers.
Who accepted as their mission
To brave their new frontiers

THE TOWER

They would toss their trash before him
As though he had no worth.
For he was just a janitor,
A station borne of birth.

He suffered their indignities
But never said a word.
A victim of misconceptions
While anger he would gird.

Though there's a secret he possessed
He felt he must conceal.
For it would give him leverage
When it he should reveal.

THE VISION

The vision that had come to him
Was tucked within a dream.
That said the world faced destruction
Beyond what they'd seen stream.

It appeared as a directive
And not just a request.
As though whatever had remained,
Their fate on him would rest.

While few had known that he'd appeared
A half a world away.
The vision in Zack's dreams had said
A threat emerged that day.

The vision that had come to him
Provided no true clue.
There was nothing too specific
To what he was to do.

It had seemed like a compulsion
That to it he was drawn.
For the vision so compelling
The quest he'd settled on.

THE OVERLORD

It's from the ashes he emerged
Or that had been his claim.
He said he was the Overlord
And knew no other name.

He paid homage to the Tower
Which he was meant to serve.
The remnants of humanity
Had been his to preserve.

The mission that was given him
Had been to resurrect
The world as it had existed
Before the war's effect.

Few at first paid him attention.
Even fewer believed
That he had been a messenger
Where hope could be retrieved.

ELI DAVIS

Eli Davis was Zack's best friend
Since they had been aged five.
He too one of the lucky ones
That somehow would survive.

He hated how they treated Zack
Believing it unfair.
For he, like all the other ones,
Was lucky to be there.

Though he had never spoken up
Against what they had done.
He'd no wish to be targeted
Where their attention won.

He had found he was embarrassed
To face his cowardice.
He had watched his best friend suffer
While feeling powerless.

He was afraid they'd turn on him
If he had said a word.
So, he watched his friend tormented
As though part of the herd.

He feared one day there'd come a time
When penance he would pay.
For when Zack most needed a friend
He'd coldly turned away.

It's said that payback is a bitch
And he would come to find
In the payback for betrayal
Justice is never blind.

THE FAITHFUL

They came to him in dribs and drabs,
All wanting something more
Than what was abject poverty
That had followed the war.

But they quickly grew in number
As word had quickly spread
The Overlord, the chosen one
By whom they would be led.

He had called the throngs the faithful
Who had received the Word.
Who hung on ev'ry syllable
That from him they had heard.

His followers were committed
To where they seemed possessed.
As they grew in their devotion
To where they seemed obsessed.

Though the faithful seemed like lemmings
Where if he should implore
They would march into the ocean
Directly from the shore.

THE QUEST

Zack challenged his community
With need of volunteers.
For he believed his quest required
Those who'd control their fears.

He declared he had a vision
Though source had been unknown.
But it was clear his destiny
Was what he had been shown.

They believed he was a madman
Who'd lost all self-control.
Whose desperation led him to
This madness to extol.

The Overlord he claimed a threat
Like none they'd known before.
For the war was just a prelude
To what he had in store.

Though he gave no explanation
He claimed behind it all
Was the structure termed the Tower
That stood unscathed and tall.

When Zack spoke of the Overlord
Most people turned away.
For with no communications
None knew the threat in play.

While most believed Zack was a fool
Who'd clearly lost his mind.
There were a few who had believed
The warning he defined.

He'd no need for the faint of heart
Or those troubled with doubt.
He needed those who would commit
To what the quest's about.

A quest that's long and arduous
Was what he had proposed.
But only three answered the call
With all the rest opposed.

Most people thought he was a fool
And possibly insane.
The quest Zack chose to undertake
Was more than just inane.

For Zack's chosen destination
Was half a world away.
Across an uncharted landscape
Where death had been in play.

THE VOLUNTEERS

Eli, the first to volunteer,
Was met with chants and jeers
To think he would align himself
In search of harsh frontiers.

Perhaps it was a sense of guilt
Or possibly his shame
That he'd never stood up for Zack
While insults Zack would claim.

Nick Johnson was an engineer
Who fell into disgrace
Because the things he prophesized
The world refused to face.

Now living in the aftermath
Nick Johnson they would shun.
For he'd been blamed for what occurred
Though nothing had he done.

Which had made him a large unknown
As to his true intent.
Zack sure Nick felt some bitterness
But not to what extent.

Zack had hoped that he could trust him
Though found he'd little choice.
There weren't that many volunteers
That brought Zack to rejoice.

The girl, though, neither one had known
But they'd seen her around.
She mainly had kept to herself
And had seemed tightly wound.

It's clear she was a warrior
As her face bore a scar.
Which strangely gave her character
And looks had failed to mar.

While she was not allowed to serve
They called her an ally.
For they had found her highly skilled
And not afraid to die.

She appeared a private person
Who rarely said a word.
She'd always seemed so serious
It bordered on absurd.

She told Zack that her name was Dawn
And she would volunteer.
For she'd found that there was nothing
That served to keep her here.

They armed themselves the best they could
With what they found on hand.
Though weapons had been plentiful,
Ammo in short demand.

While vehicles were obsolete
With fuel supplies destroyed.
Their journey would be arduous
As on foot they deployed.

THE QUEST BEGINS

The four basic'ly were strangers
With trust in short supply.
Zack assumed each had a reason
They'd risk the chance to die.

The landscape was a mystery
For which they must prepare.
The quest would be a lengthy one
With danger ev'rywhere.

Though they found it was a challenge
That showed them no respect.
For in their current circumstance
Knew not what to expect.

Though he knew there'd be diversions
He'd no way to have known
How dangerous would be the quest
When facing the unknown.

The first night out, when they made camp,
No small talk was enjoyed.
It seemed suspicions still ran high
Which left them all annoyed.

While they ate their meal in silence,
The only thing they shared.
For none had wished to open up
As though they had not dared.

While clearly at the journey's start
It became obvious
The new state of the After World
Had grown more hazardous.

For none of them possessed a clue
To what they could expect.
For in terms of the After World
Life was shown no respect.

THE QUESTIONING

Zack began to question motives
To why they volunteered.
For Zack could tell they weren't convinced
In quest he engineered.

Although they all had chose this path
They'd no chance of success
If trust was not an element
That each of them would bless.

Their lives would be in jeopardy
If they could not rely
That the others would have their back
If danger should draw nigh.

They needed to develop trust
If they were to survive.
For otherwise the quest they're on
They'd not finish alive.

FIRST ENCOUNTER

The first few days uneventful
Though progress had been slow.
For they saw no need to hurry
Cross terrain they'd not know.

It was Eli who first saw it
And thankfully he did.
It was some type of booby trap
That cleverly was hid.

Zack warned them all to be on guard.
Someone must be close by.
It clearly was no accident
Someone wished them to die.

When he charged from the underbrush,
He caught them by surprise.
While the guys had dove for cover
Dawn stared him in the eyes.

They saw he was a hulking man
Who stood about six five.
He clearly had looked menacing
And meant to stay alive.

When Dawn ordered him to stand down
His face showed puzzlement.
She'd not seemed a superior
Though message clearly sent.

SOLDIER

His parents had abandoned him
When he was just a lad.
His parents' death an accident
That left him scarred and mad.

Thus, love had been unknown to him
As he lived on the street
Until the day they captured him
With future forced to meet.

Like other orphans he was trained
Especially for war.
He'd no other identity
As death he was trained for.

So, Soldier was the only name
That he had ever known
And kindness was a luxury
That he was never shown.

A battle-tested veteran
Who'd cheated death so far.
Who'd been a liability.
As age his skills would mar.

He'd little personality
And rarely had he spoke.
He possessed no sense of humor
Thus, immune to a joke.

They asked Soldier to go with them
Where he'd not be alone.
Then Zack informed him of the quest
Which Soldier too could own.

It was Soldier who informed them
Of what he called the plague.
But the words had seemed to fail him
Thus, warning had been vague.

THE PLAGUE

He'd seen them on their pilgrimage
And known they were a threat.
For they'd displayed no sense of fear
Nor challenge went unmet.

The faithful proved to be a plague
That no one had foreseen.
With devotion that's limitless
Like none the world had seen.

His message seemed to speak to those
Who had abandoned hope.
As though he was a drug pusher
And all hooked on his dope.

For it seemed with their conversion
Came a loss of free will.
Replaced with a single purpose
To his wishes fulfill.

They were like a horde of zombies
That were his to command.
As though they had become diseased
In which he'd had a hand.

Where once conversion was complete
There was no going back.
For this had stretched beyond a cult
As faith would never slack.

The message of the Overlord
Had been spread like a plague.
For, though he rallied followers,
His message had been vague.

THE MARSH

Though the marsh had looked forbidding
There was no other course.
For the marsh appeared extensive
Which left them no recourse.

The vegetation had been dense
Which made the going slow.
Not to mention they were wary
What from the marsh may show.

They heard it long before it pounced
Though they were still surprised.
It's clear it had been stalking them
With its attack devised.

Clearly, an abomination
That God never designed.
A product of the After World
That had been redefined.

Though not identifiable
To what it once had been
The creature showed a clear intent
A meal it meant to win.

A claw caught Nick across the chest
As Zack pushed Nick away.
Then Dawn it seemed it targeted
On whom it wished to prey. Though

Eli shot the creature twice
It showed no ill effect.
It simply turned and charged again
Which they did not expect.

When Dawn had moved to intercede,
Soldier pushed her aside.
Then from his belt he pulled a knife
As Dawn watched them collide.

The struggle had been touch and go
With no advantage gained.
When Soldier had rose to his feet
Though completely bloodstained.

Nick's wound had been more serious
Than they at first believed.
Where they knew he'd need attention
Beyond what he'd received.

Perhaps the trust for which Zack wished
Had now come into play.
They worked together as a team
With creature theirs to slay.

They found a medic to treat Nick
In next encampment found.
They told Soldier to stay with Nick
While they would search around.

FINDING PIPER

They found Piper in Bordertown
Whose body was for sale.
They claimed she was a criminal
Who refused to post bail.

They saw her struggle with her chains
Unwilling to submit.
Defiantly she screamed at them
Then at the crowd had spit.

Zack was confused by what he'd seen
And found his stomach turned.
It seemed that in the After World
No lessons had been learned.

Zack bought her freedom with two guns
And half a dozen rounds.
But when they handed him the leash
Her anger knew no bounds.

Where she viciously attacked him
While he was caught off guard.
And though he tried to calm her down
Attempt she'd disregard.

When he told her he would free her
Composure she reclaimed.
And yet, he found he was intrigued
With what she had been blamed.

She'd shown no sense of gratitude
That by him she was freed.As
though she had expected it
And thus had seen no need.

He told her she was free to go
Or she could choose to stay.
He really did not give a damn
What happened either way.

Dawn invited her to join them
Which Zack strongly opposed.
Then Eli seconded her request
Where Zack felt he was hosed.

She was almost schizophrenic
The way her moods would change.
He'd seen her at her very worse
Which brought to mind derange.

She said her welcome had run out
With no place else to go.
Perhaps their quest a welcomed change
From what she'd come to know.

It's clear the woman was a bitch
Who'd go out of her way
To create a mass disturbance
Then simply walk away.

Zack believed she'd be a problem
If she should join the quest.
So, he had been a bit disturbed
His concerns weren't addressed.

ELI'S DISCOVERY

It's Eli's smile that worried Zack
For he'd not smiled a lot.
While the satchel Eli carried
Had not been hard to spot.

For Eli looked pleased with himself
And thus the stupid grin.
While Zack was more than hesitant
To ask what lurked within.

Then Eli said that he'd obtained
Some weapons tried and true.
They may look to be medieval
Though in a pinch they'd do.

It's then he had unveiled his stash
That glistened in the sun.
The weapons were antiquities
But none had been a gun.

When Zack asked where he had found them
Eli calmly replied
He'd found them in a refuse pile
Where they'd been cast aside.

Though Zack admired initiative
He had not understood
What's the use of swords and crossbows
That to them would prove good?

THE DESERT

As they took leave of Bordertown
One question still remained.
The direction they should travel
If quest to be maintained.

It had stretched vast and expensive
And seemed to have no end.
Piper said it once was forest
But war saw it descend.

For the forest now a desert
Both desolate and bare.
Which most likely had its secrets
That they'd be forced to dare.

As they set out, Dawn took the lead,
While Soldier took the rear.
The rest assembled in between
And carried all their gear.

Each dune they struggled to assail.
Led to another one.
And all the while the searing heat
Beat on them from the sun.

The nights, though, had been freezing cold
With no chance of a fire.
They found extremes unbearable
That grew to a quagmire.

Zack had noticed Piper's pendant
That she'd kiss ev'ry night.
As if its blessed with properties
That were beyond his sight.

It seemed to be a ritual
She followed ev'ry night
But she tried to keep it secret
And did it out of sight.

Their journey grew monotonous
As nothing seemed to change.
For ev'ry dune that they would climb
Another came in range.

PIPER'S ADMISSION

Although he never trusted her
Zack found he was surprised
To find her sitting in the sand
Where tears had filled her eyes.

He started to just walk away
But found that he could not.
While clear that Piper was distressed
He could not leave the spot.

Though as he sat down next to her,
She tried to turn away.
He placed a hand on her shoulder
To tell her it's okay.

When he asked what had troubled her,
She merely shook her head.
Zack worried he may be the cause
By something that he'd said.

His hand remained on her shoulder
As she had grown composed.
Yet, she still had told him nothing
Where troubles were disclosed.

Again, he asked what's the matter
But she said not a word.
She simply stared across the sand
As though she had not heard.

But when he rose as if to leave
She begged him not to go.
For her secrets truly shamed her
And best he did not know.

Then pendant she would fiddle with
Whenever she would speak.
He wondered its significance
But answers did not seek.

So, he again sat next to her
Where silence was maintained.
Though Zack had a thousand questions,
To ask not entertained.

For he thought when she was ready
In him, she may confide.
As she'd told him she had secrets
Which she chose not to hide.

Zack found he'd still not trusted her
But also had been moved.
She's not the bitch he thought she was
As that thought was removed.

A LOOMING THREAT

It seemed to be another dune
Like those they'd climbed before.
When Dawn had fallen to her knees
Which shook them to their core.

When they cautiously had joined her
They too froze in their fright.
For from their vantage point they saw
A truly ugly sight.

Many scientists prophesized
That they would outlive man.
Before them stood the evidence
Of what seemed nature's plan.

They saw they were extremely fast
When they were on attack.
With the faithful as their target
Who'd refused to fight back.

Except they were the size of wolves
And showed no sign of fear
They appeared man's superior
That they dared not go near.

They knew they were a looming threat
They clearly must avoid.
For they were clearly predators
Who of mercy devoid.

Instead, they backed away from them
Where a new path was found.
They weren't about to tempt their fate
But roaches went around.

ZACK'S SECOND VISION

The vision that awakened him
Had woke him with a start.
Zack wiped away some beads of sweat
And tried to calm his heart.

It seemed his screams woke the others
Who had rushed to his side.
Eli asked if he'd a vision
Where yes what Zack replied.

He said he'd seen the Overlord
From the Tower emerge.
And he'd floated above the ground
As 'round him they would surge.

He said he was the chosen one
Who had been born to lead.
The faithful hung on ev'ry word
As each command they'd heed.

The faithful clear to recognize
As they appeared half dead.
As if it was the Overlord
Who on their souls had fed.

Then stood before a world destroyed
And wondered what was next.
What tragedies were yet to come
To leave survivors vexed.

They all had simply stared at him
In puzzlement and awe.
As none of them were comforted
By what he said he saw.

A PROCESSION OF THE FAITHFUL

They saw them from atop a dune
Streaming across the sand.
A procession of the faithful
As if by some command.

The image that was given them
They first thought a mirage.
For the desert had its secrets
That very few could dodge.

The March seemed their single focus
As they showed no concern
For any comrade who'd collapsed
As none would stop or turn.

When they saw the swarm of roaches
They feared what was to come.
The column seemed a sitting duck
To what they would become.

The column seemed oblivious
To threat the insects posed.
They took no evasive action
Although they were exposed.

It seemed that death had been no threat
To those already dead.
The roaches took their fill of them
As they upon them fed.

There were no screams that they had heard
Nor effort to fight back.
It had seemed they were accepting
To suffer the attack.

All six of them were horrified
To see what had occurred.
But the column never wavered
Despite what it endured.

Eli asked what were they thinking,
If they had thought at all.
Their comrades killed or carried off
But column did not stall.

THE VISION CONFIRMATION

When once the column had moved on
And roaches disappeared.
They went to search for survivors
Who were not commandeered.

Nick said he found one still alive
Who was in a bad way.
They had hoped he'd give them answers
Before he passed away.

The smell was indescribable
Reeking of rotting flesh.
While his eyes had been receded
And breath was less than fresh.

When Dawn had asked him for his name—
Of name he had no need.
His master was the Overlord
For whom he'd gladly bleed.

Then he told them he'd been summoned
And tried to crawl away.
Despite his many injuries
The summons could not sway.

It had been too much for Piper
Who'd quickly turned away.
Who buried her head in Zack's chest
Though had nothing to say.

While they all were pretty shaken,
What they'd seen had confirmed
That at least part of Zack's vision
Had clearly been affirmed.

Then Nick had an epiphany
Where quest could be fulfilled.
The procession they could follow
Though option had not thrilled.

When the other four had left them
Zack asked if she's okay.
But the look that Piper gave him
Had made him turn away.

THE ONSET OF DOUBT

Although Zack was still committed
He saw the others' doubt.
He'd need to know who stood with him
And who had wanted out.

In the horror of the moment
The questioning began.
What was the purpose of the quest
And did Zack have a plan?

Though Zack not a religious man
He'd felt a need to pray.
For the answers they were seeking
He'd not bring himself to say.

It would be a hard decision
But one that must be made.
Zack needed to know who'd go on
And who was too afraid.

They each turned to one another
To see where each had stood.
Though the quest brought them together
Though unsure that was good.

Then Eli said the point was moot
As they had come too far.
They're past the point of no return
Not knowing where they are.

RELATIONSHIPS

Whenever they would look for them
Neither one could they find.
Eli and Nick would disappear
To which the rest weren't blind.

They all noticed the attraction
But none had said a word.
Whatever feelings they possessed
Had been theirs to shepherd.

Soldier and Dawn were obvious
With feelings they would show.
Although they would delude themselves
The others did not know.

Which only left Piper and Zack
Who'd not seen eye to eye.
Who'd not agreed on anything
As neither wished to try.

They knew that Zack resented her
But none were quite sure why.
It seemed if they'd not rescued her
She had been meant to die.

Their disputes became an issue
The others wished addressed.
They argued about ev'rything
Where the rest grew distressed.

It seemed their constant bickering
Had sometimes seemed contrived.
As though there's something between them
That suddenly arrived.

A MEETING OF THE MINDS

Zack wandered off to be alone
And ponder what occurred.
He'd found it more than troubling
Death may have been deferred.

Piper found Zack by accident
As she'd not gone to look.
She too had wished some solitude
Because her hands still shook.

Somehow he knew that she was there
But had not turned around.
Though she thought she had been stealthy
And had not made a sound.

The invitation offered her
She found hard to reject.
So, she had sat down next to him
Unsure what to expect.

While they sat in total silence,
Piper summoned the nerve
To ask Zack about the visions
And purpose that they serve.

The question had caught Zack off guard
As he had questions too.
But thought she deserved an answer
After what they'd been through.

Whatever had been guiding him
Only spoke through his dreams.
But he never got a warning
Before a vision streams.

Zack said whomever spoke to him
He believed was divine.
For it had not directed him
To cross a moral line.

But the visions never told him
What part they were to play.
It just said to find the Tower
And helped him find the way.

He knew it seemed incredible
But it had been a fact.
The visions gave him direction
On which he had to act.

Then with Piper's question answered,
An answer Zack thought due.
So asked Piper why she joined them
When none of them she knew.

It was nothing she was proud of
But she'd been desperate.
So, sold the only thing she had
With hunger to offset.

But with the choice lost self-respect
And a part of her soul.
Then shunned by the community
O'er which she'd no control.

That was why she was so eager
To join them on their quest.
For she found death preferable
To life she would divest.

Then she thanked him for his kindness
As she had stood to leave.
For so little had been shown her
That was not make-believe.

As Zack watched Piper walk away
He found that he had stared.
A moment of civility
The two of them had shared.

Zack had felt a certain feeling
He had no wish to feel.
Where he had loathed to recognize
The feeling had been real.

Gordon Bostic

THE FIRST DOWN PAYMENT

The cockroaches, intelligent,
Who too followed the March.
For they had found a food supply
And made a countermarch.

The March left a trail of bodies
Thus was easy to track.
But while they kept the March in sight
The six of them hung back.

When they found they had a problem
With what they'd have to deal.
If left unchecked, the roaches would
All of the faithful kill.

Nick said time to get medieval
As he brandished a sword.
Though feared that they faced certain death
As manner of reward.

Zack told Dawn to follow the March
While they would make a stand.
And later they'd catch up to her
When the threat they'd disband.

Piper deadly with a crossbow
Which came as a surprise.
They'd not seen her a warrior
Which maybe was unwise.

Soldier proved he's the warrior
That he had claimed to be
As he jumped amid the roaches
With abject savagery.

Armed with a sword in both his hands
Soldier had slashed and stabbed.
While the roaches were persistent
Soldier had hacked and jabbed.

While the others had done their part
He fought like a machine.
Where the roaches had grown wary
Till most had fled the scene.

One had breached their perimeter
Which had produced a scream.
They saw Nick trapped within its jaws
Thus, to his aid, they'd stream.

When a life hangs in the balance
Most people just react.
And don't always think that clearly
Which is a simple fact.

In a fit of rage, Eli attacked
Though it had been too late.
For Nick already had succumbed
To his undeserved fate.

But Zack intercepted Eli
Before death took him too.
While Soldier had dispatched the roach
By cleaving it in two.

Eli was inconsolable
Though Piper really tried.
Which Zack had not failed to notice
The compassion applied.

It was in that fateful moment
They came to recognize
Just how grave their situation
And how close their demise.

THE ACCUSATIONS

There had been no sense of closure
When closure was desired.
As they could not afford the time
They thought may be required.

The accusations Eli made
The rest thought undeserved.
For Zack was not who murdered Nick
Though all had been unnerved.

Zack stood alone in his self-doubt
As Eli had been right.
For he's the one who'd called to them
Thus, reason for their plight.

The guilt had made him feel ashamed
That he got them involved.
The visions never warned him of
A guilt gone unreserved.

Then Piper came to Zack's defense
To say it was unfair.
As Zack was not responsible
For state of the affair.

While each had joined the quest by choice
Where risks were clearly known.
Now when those risks they had to face
That choice they would disown.

They're wasting time assigning blame
Where no blame could be found.
It merely was the circumstance
To which they had been bound.

Though Eli then apologized
It had not seemed heartfelt.
He'd harbored animosity
For hand that he'd been dealt.

THE JUNGLE

From the desert rose a jungle
That appeared lush and green.
Though feared the threats awaiting them
That had yet to be seen.

The trail they found not hard to find
With vegetation mashed.
Although no bodies had they found
Though foliage was trashed.

When they at last caught up to Dawn
They found she was amazed.
She said the March unstoppable
As they could not be fazed.

They must've numbered in the thousands
When the March had begun.
Then bolstered by reinforcements
They now had marched as one.

Even vegetation altered
As a result of war.
Where what once had seemed so docile
Had now become much more.

The vegetation was alive
And many were consumed.
But the March had never halted
To help those who were doomed.

The vines encircled Piper's legs
And pulled her to the ground.
But thanks to Soldier's quick response
Her freedom again found.

The vines had come from ev'rywhere
Where despite how they'd hack.
They barely had resisted them
Or thwarted their attack.

For reasons Piper couldn't explain
Zack jumped in front of her
To use his body as a shield
So harm he could deter.

Although a courageous gesture
She could appreciate.
She was not sure she's worthy of
A risk that was so great.

Dawn told the rest to hold them off
As strips from her shirt ripped.
She wrapped the strips around her sword
Then to a match she tipped.

The vines would not approach the flame
So, by a path she led.
Until they had been clear of them
And plants had gone unfed.

THE BRIDGE TO STILL WATER

Once they thought that they'd reached safety
They stopped to take a break.
And thanked Dawn's ingenuity
That exit they could make.

Piper proved to be much stronger
Than Zack thought she would be.
For she accepted what occurred
Much better than had he.

Piper felt Zack's eyes upon her
So turned to him and smiled.
Gone was the animosity
That once before beguiled.

In the distance they heard gunfire
That had seemed out of place.
While unsure of its origin
Towards it began to race.

As they approached, they saw the bridge
On which bodies were piled.
It looked as though a massacre
The way the bodies styled.

The bridge had led to Still Water
According to the sign.
But found that it was littered with
Those dead or in decline.

The bodies were of the faithful
Till the bridge's far side.
It's there they found the citizens
Who'd tried to stem the tide.

They worked their way across the bridge
Where they were forced to meet
The residents of Still Water
Who had tasted defeat.

They said it was a tidal wave
That cross the bridge had flowed.
And though they'd shot them by the score
The wave had never slowed.

There were no weapons they possessed
As there had been no need.
With numbers so superior
Progress could not impede.

The savagery that was displayed
Had come as a surprise.
For ev'ry time they'd been observed
The March was all they'd prize.

But when the March it seemed was blocked
Their demeanor had changed.
No longer were they pacifists
But instead grew deranged.

When Zack explained about the quest
They offered them reprieve.
Where they could try renew themselves
Before they chose to leave.

STILL WATER

They found respite in Still Water
Where they could rest and heal.
Its people had been generous
And kind in their appeal.

Each was given their own quarters
And had been fully fed.
Then for the first time in some months
Had been granted a bed.

They helped them to restore their camp
Which the March left a mess.
As there was extensive damage
The townsfolk must address.

Gordon Bostic

They then helped remove the bodies
And to bury their dead.
Then reassured the citizens
They'd nothing more to dread.

In the evening, they told stories
Of what they'd seen and done.
Though played down the graphic details
As they'd no wish to stun.

The people made them feel at home
But knew they could not stay.
For the quest still laid before them
They could not long delay.

72

THE LAKE

Still Water stood beside a lake
They said was fresh and clean.
As the flora surrounding it
Had remained lush and green.

Their children swam there all the time
Without an incident.
They all believed the lake was safe
If swimming their intent.

The water looked so inviting
They just could not resist.
The thought of being clean again
Was reason to exist.

Piper and Dawn had demanded
They have some privacy.
As both had wished to take a bath
The others need not see.

So, they had gone around the lake
To find a private spot.
For neither wished to be ogled
Nor when naked be caught.

Though they found the lake refreshing
There was an eerie feel.
As though someone was watching them
Which both thought was surreal.

By the time that they had seen it
It almost was too late.
They saw it bearing down on them
But had chose not to wait.

It may once have been a gator
But it was hard to tell.
Because the thing was so deformed
It must have come from hell.

They were completely defenseless
In face of its approach.
So, both began to scream for help
In lieu of its encroach.

They swam as hard as they could swim
But they were losing ground.
The creature quickly gained on them
Believing dinner found.

They heard the splash but had not seen
Who'd come to their rescue.
It seemed like an eternity
Till Zack came into view.

A crowd had formed along the shore
To watch it all unfold.
Where they all gasped in amazement
Of one who was that bold.

He saw directly at the thing
With only knife in hand.
They feared it may be suicide
That Zack had deftly planned.

When they reached shore, Piper and Dawn
Had from the lake climbed free.
While neither one concerned themselves
With thoughts of modesty.

Though its jaws were terrifying
Zack did not hesitate.
He stabbed the creature in the eye
As he had tempted fate.

The creature flailed in agony
Before it disappeared.
As Zack calmly returned to shore
Where he was wildly cheered.

A LIFETIME IN AN EVENING

In a moment of reflection
She stood outside his door.
He twice had risked his life for her
Which she could not ignore.

She did not know how much he knew
Or if he felt the same.
But she thought it's now or never
If his heart hers to claim.

Zack woke to Piper standing there
As her clothes she'd remove.
She told him if she was to die
Her love she wished to prove.

THE TOWER

He did not wait for her to come
But went to her instead.
Then lifted her into his arms
And carried her to bed.

Not knowing what the sun may bring
Or how long they may last.
In that night, they lived a lifetime
Unmindful of the past.

Although they thought they'd been discreet
The rest had clearly known.
For there had been a change in them
That they had clearly shown.

THE PENDANT

The only thing Piper valued
Was the pendant she wore.
For it once had been her mother's
Whom she'd always adore.

So, when she offered it to Zack
He truly had been moved.
But he gently had refused it
As it she had removed.

It was a gift he'd not accept
While knowing what it meant.
For he thought he was unworthy
Of message that was sent.

But she wanted him to have it
To show he'd claimed her heart.
The only thing that she possessed
Of which she'd felt a part.

She placed the piece around his neck
And kissed him on the cheek.
For if something was to happen
The piece for her could speak.

It was more than just a gesture
He'd seen it in her eyes.
For without words, Piper told him
Their love she'd come to prize.

THE THIRD VISION

Again, his screams had pierced the night
To force them all awake.
Another vision came to him
Which brought his heart to ache.

The entire camp had been alarmed
When they heard Zack cry out.
As most of them had been unnerved
To find what it's about.

The Overlord was not the threat
Zack once thought him to be.
But extension of the Tower
In its reality.

The Tower knew they were coming
Thus, it would be prepared.
There was no chance of a surprise
For that was now impaired.

It would not sit and wait for them
As their purpose it knew.
Assured it would defend itself
When any threat came due.

THE DEMONS IN HIS MIND

Zack heard the door slowly open
Then saw someone slip in.
But in the darkness could not tell
Whoever it had been.

At first, he thought Piper returned
But something had felt wrong.
The steps were way too hesitant
And seemed to be too strong.

Zack steeled himself for what's to come
So, he'd not be surprised.
He'd felt someone was stalking him
And danger recognized.

When the intruder had attacked
Zack found himself prepared
The knife he held, Zack had restrained
Where possession they shared.

The two then struggled on the floor,
Each with their own intent.
As Zack had fought to stay alive.
The other murder meant.

The struggle heard by most of camp
Who ran to view the fray.
But when the first had reached the scene
They found things weren't okay.

For Eli laid dead on the floor
While Zack had held the knife.
It seemed that he was traumatized
To take his best friend's life.

Piper and Dawn both ran to Zack
When they had seen the blood.
Zack's wound, they feared, was serious
As it had seemed to flood.

Zack then muttered half consciously
He could not understand.
Why would Eli want to kill him?
As Piper took his hand.

Perhaps he'd not forgiven Zack,
Piper softly replied.
And still held him accountable
As reason Nick had died.

If his grief was all-consuming
And closure could not find.
The only thing Eli had left
Were demons in his mind.

A RETURN TO THE QUEST

Zack was slow in his recovery
As his wound had been deep.
And the reoccurring nightmares
Had made it hard to sleep.

But he'd felt the reservations
Where no one wished to leave.
Unsure of what awaited them
Beyond what they'd conceive.

For they had found a comfort zone
Where acceptance was won.
With fear if they left Still Water
Their lives most likely done.

It seemed that death was stalking them
Or they'd been singled out.
Perhaps it was a lack of luck
As luck they'd been without.

As they made their preparations
To return to the quest
They had thanked their hosts profusely
For treating them as guest.

The trail would not be hard to find
From what they'd seen before.
For the swath of devastation
Difficult to restore.

THE ENCAMPMENT

When they saw the old encampment
They truly had no clue
What it was they had stumbled on
Or trouble they were due.

All at once, they were surrounded
Where each possessed a gun.
The four of them truly believed
That they were surely done.

They had found a small contingent
Of troops left from the war.
Who had seemed to be forgotten
With nothing to fight for.

When the Sergeant had approached them
His look was more than stern.
He then asked how they had found them
Which seemed of great concern.

Then when his eyes fell on Soldier
His face lit with a smile.
For at one time they were comrades
He'd not seen in a while.

The troops next lowered their weapons
Though tensions were preserved.
Soldier said Sarge was a buddy
With whom he twice had served.

Soldier told them what had happened
And of the After World.
Then Zack informed them of the quest
To try to save their world.

Soldier asked Sarge why they were here
And how long had they been.
For it seemed an odd location
That they'd been staged within.

THE TOWER

Sarge said it was the area
They're assigned to defend.
But were given no new orders
Since the war reached an end.

Next, Zack asked about the Tower
And if Sarge had a clue
To where the Tower may have stood
Where way he'd point them to.

Sarge had known about the Tower
As rumors he had heard.
But the trek would not be easy
Unless he was a bird.

With no need of military
They'd nothing else to do.
Perhaps they'd join them on their quest
And see their mission through.

THE MOUNTAINS

When the mountains stretched before them
It filled them with concern.
For the view had been imposing
Yet, from them could not turn.

They proved to be an obstacle
For which they weren't prepared.
As three of them were hesitant
If not just downright scared.

When Piper looked into Zack's eyes
She saw he was afraid.
So, she had kissed him long and hard
Before ascent was made.

The troops were more experienced
Thus, they'd taken the lead.
The other four would follow them
With their advice to heed.

The footing had been treacherous
And all were well-aware
That any misstep may result
In clutching at thin air.

The cold was indescribable
The higher they had gone.
Where movement had grown difficult
Though, still, they had pushed on.

The stones beneath Dawn's feet had slipped
And balance she had lost.
When Soldier had reached out to her
Unmindful of the cost.

Then Soldier too was compromised
As his legs had gone stiff.
Then he and Dawn had both been lost
As they went off the cliff.

Next, as the two had disappeared
Piper let out a scream.
She cried, "This can't be happening!
It had to be a dream!"

Now only two of them remained
Who had begun the quest.
As death had been the true reward
Awarded to the rest.

The descent had been no better
Than had been the ascent.
The footing still was treacherous
They could not circumvent.

They'd chosen to be more cautious
Which also took more time.
Another soldier had been killed
While on the downhill climb.

The city they saw in descent
Looked desolate and bare.
Which was once a gleaming wonder
That reveled in its flair.

But when they reached the mountain's base
They had felt great relief.
Although what still laid before them
Was sure to bring them grief.

ZACK'S FOURTH VISION

This time, the vision came to him
While he was wide-awake.
And chilled him to his very core
With what had been at stake.

Their souls were what it wished of them
And wanted nothing more.
For the purpose of the Tower
Had been served by the war.

The faithful nothing more than drones
Who hearkened to its will.
The Overlord had been a sham
That it used as a shill.

The Tower, the epicenter
Of all that had occurred.
At its core the Tower evil
Where the truth it had blurred.

He'd thought it was the Overlord
Whom they were meant to fear.
But the vision said the Tower
Was what he'd need to clear.

IN LIGHT OF WHAT THEY'D SEEN

With the city laid before them
They were without a plan.
They needed a high vantage point
Where city they could scan.

They saw nothing more than rubble
As the result of war.
Although the Tower stood unscathed
As if war was planned for.

Sarge motioned them to follow him
To vantage point he'd found.
Where the city sprawled beneath them
And they could look around.

It stood as though a monolith
That knew not time or age.
A structure built of true mystique
That few would dare engage.

They had seen it was encircled
By a retaining wall.
Where access had been limited
To almost one and all.

THE TOWER

The wall had seemed unscalable
But had possessed one gate.
Which was under a heavy guard
Of faithful numbered eight.

Then they saw the faithful gathered
Before the Overlord.
Who had numbered in the thousands
As a true lethal horde.

The Tower was unreachable
In light of what they'd seen.
The faithful were a massive force
That had stood in between.

The quest now seemed impossible
From all that they had seen.
For the Tower was a fortress
Which Zack had not foreseen.

Gordon Bostic

SECOND THOUGHTS

Though Piper wanted to turn back
Zack would not hear of it.
As with the quest he was obsessed
Which he would not admit.

She found she had no wish to die
At least, not anymore.
As she had been in love with Zack
With something to live for.

He'd become much like the faithful
In purpose and desire.
As though nothing else had mattered
Till the quest should expire.

Piper feared that Zack's obsession
Would lead to his demise
He'd been so driven by the quest
His acts not always wise.

GOING UNDERGROUND

They'd no way to reach the Tower
By going aboveground.
But Sarge said that there were tunnels
That had run underground.

Though largely inaccessible
Due to war and decay.
Where many of the exit points
He feared may not give way.

But Zack had seen no other way
If quest he'd to complete.
It was a risk he had to take
Despite what fate he'd meet.

The others, though, were not required
To go where he must go.
Yet, when he laid it out for them
There're none who had said no.

Zack took her in his arms and said
That she should stay behind.
There was no way that they could know
What dangers they may find.

Piper said if she's to lose him
She may as well be dead.
So, she was going where he went
Despite what laid ahead.

They waited till it had grown dark
When they made their descent.
With less chance of discovery
When they made their ascent.

The tunnels were like catacombs
The way they'd twist and turn.
So, they'd not found a direct path
Which caused them some concern.

It seemed that fate was kind to them
When exit point was reached.
They only prayed that it still worked
And exit could be breached.

Though the journey took much longer
Than Zack at first had thought.
So, when they reached their exit point
In sunlight, they were caught.

THE SECRETS OF THE TOWER

When from the tunnels they emerged
They had been quickly spied.
Their timing had been horrible
And had no place to hide.

The Tower had stood yards away
Where they were forced to run.
The faithful were unleashed on them
Where they thought they were done.

They killed the faithful at the gate
Then forced their way inside.
Where they closed the gate behind them
To stem the growing tide.

Sarge promised Zack they'd hold the gate
For as long as they could.
So, the two could breach the Tower
And try to do some good.

The faithful surged against the gate
While crushing those in front.
The Overlord had urged them on
With intruders to hunt.

Sarge told his troops to hold their fire
Until the gate gave way.
For they lacked the ammunition
To all the faithful slay.

As the gate finally gave way
The troops had opened fire
But with their numbers overwhelming
The situation dire.

While the troop's screams had been haunting
The faithful gave no pause.
The savagery that was displayed
By hands made into claws.

When they'd heard gunfire from outside
Zack then bolted the door.
Piper begged him not to do it
Which he chose to ignore.

She said Sarge and all the others
Would all be trapped outside.
If he should deny them access
By locking them inside.

Though she thought she understood him,
She clearly had no clue.
For the man she had been paired with
Was one she never knew.

For their presence in the Tower
Had sparked in Zack a change.
She'd thought he'd grown irrational
Or at least acted strange.

It had seemed the quest consumed him
While she had knelt and cried.
For Zack had seemed oblivious
That all the others died

Their friends had sacrificed themselves
Where they'd have the chance
To eradicate the Tower
Or its demise advance.

Her safety was his first concern.
The Tower had been next.
Then saw in the interior
What had left them perplexed.

It possessed a spiral staircase
That ran along its wall.
With a plethora of doorways
That were both large and small.

In the first door that he opened
He saw a world destroyed.
There had not been a sign of life,
If life was once deployed.

A second door showed much the same,
A wasteland dead and bare.
A world that seemed so desolate
It had no need of air.

The Tower was a conduit
That led to other worlds.
A gateway to apocalypse
Where only chaos swirls.

They then looked to one another
And in that moment knew
That they must destroy the Tower
Though it had known it too.

All the doors at once blew open
Where they could hear the cries.
A thousand worlds in their death throes
Alarmed at their demise.

Then one door had spawned a vortex
That tried to pull Zack in.
He had grabbed hold of the doorframe
To not be sucked within.

Though Piper wrapped him in her arms
The pull had been too strong.
She found she had to let him go
Or she'd be pulled along.

While Piper had reached out to him
Zack had been pulled away.
He heard Piper call out to him
With alarm to convey.

EPILOGUE

Zack woke to see the orderly
Present him with his med.
But when he tried to reach for it
He'd been strapped to his bed.

Diagnosed as delusional
Zack had to be restrained.
He lived a life of fantasy
Only his mind contained.

They'd not believe a thing he said
As they could not be sure
If he had even known the truth
As truth to him obscure.

He'd regale the staff with stories
Fantastic and bizarre.
The staff had thought impossible
That left their mouths ajar.

But they would dismiss his stories
As purely fictional.
He'd not left the institution
And rarely rational.

When he told them of the Tower
None paid him any mind
Nor had noticed his new pendant
To which they had been blind.

ABOUT THE AUTHOR

Gordon Bostic was born in West Virginia and grew up in Virginia. A graduate of James Madison University and Fairleigh Dickinson University, he worked as a computer scientist and a software engineer for most of his life. He began writing at a young age as a way of expressing himself, his feelings and his view of the world. Gordon has also had an interest in telling his stories in one way or another. "The Walk" is his sixth novel. Gordon currently lives on the Jersey Shore with his wife, Susan.